OLSAT® Practice Test for Fourth and Fifth Grade

Book Cover by: Carol Hampshire
Illustrations by: Mirona Jova
Written and published by: Bright Kids NYC

The Otis-Lennon School Ability Test (OLSAT®) is a registered trademark of NCS Pearson Inc. Pearson Inc. neither endorses nor supports the content of the OLSAT® Practice Test.

Bright Kids NYC Inc.
225 Broadway, Suite 3104
New York, NY 10007
www.brightkidsnyc.com
www.twitter.com/brightkidsnyc
info@brightkidsnyc.com
917-539-4575

Table of Contents

OLSAT® Practice Test for Fourth and Fifth Grade

Bright Kids NYC Inc. ©

About Bright Kids NYC

Bright Kids NYC was founded in New York City to provide language arts and math enrichment for young children and to educate parents about standardized tests through workshops and consultations, as well as to prepare young children for such tests through assessments, tutoring and publications. Our philosophy is that regardless of age, test-taking is a skill that can be acquired and mastered through practice.

At Bright Kids NYC, we strive to provide the best learning materials. Our publications are truly unique. First, all of our books have been created by qualified psychologists, learning specialists and teachers. Second, our books have been tested by hundreds of children in our tutoring practice. Since children can make associations that many adults cannot, testing of materials by children is critical to creating successful test preparation guides. Finally, our learning specialists and teaching staff have provided practical strategies and tips so parents can best help their child prepare to compete successfully on standardized tests.

Feel free to contact us should you have any questions.

Bright Kids NYC Inc.

225 Broadway, Suite 3104
New York, New York, 10007

Phone: 917-539-4575

Email: info@brightkidsnyc.com

www.brightkidsnyc.com

www.twitter.com/brightkidsnyc

Introduction

Bright Kids NYC created the OLSAT® Practice Test to familiarize children with the content and the format of the OLSAT®. Children, no matter how bright they are, do not always perform well when they are not accustomed to the format and the structure of a test. Children can misunderstand the directions, fail to consider all the answer choices, and may not always read the questions carefully. Thus, without adequate preparation and familiarization, children may not always perform to the best of their ability on standardized tests such as the OLSAT®.

This Bright Kids NYC OLSAT® Practice Test is not designed to generate a score or a percentile rank as the test has not been standardized with the actual OLSAT® norms and standards. The objective of the practice test is to identify your child's strengths, weaknesses and overall test taking ability so that you can prepare your child adequately for the actual test. The Answer Key includes the question type so that you can easily identify what type of OLSAT® questions your child is struggling with and the explanations provided will aid you in making sure the concepts are grasped.

In order to maximize the effectiveness of the Bright Kids NYC OLSAT® Practice Test, it is important to first familiarize yourself with the test and its instructions. In addition, it is recommended that you designate a quiet place to work with your child, ideally in a neutral environment free of noise and clutter. Finally, provide a comfortable and a proper seating arrangement to enable your child to focus and concentrate to the best of his or her ability.

Children will be taking many standardized tests throughout their school years. Teaching your child critical thinking skills along with test taking strategies will benefit your child for many years to come.

OLSAT® Overview

The Otis-Lennon School Ability Test® (OLSAT®) was discovered and published in 1918 by Dr. Arthur Otis who was completing graduate work at Stanford University. The Otis Group Intelligence Scale was followed by the Otis Self-Administering Tests of Mental Ability, the Otis Quick-Scoring Mental Ability Tests, the Otis-Lennon Mental Ability Test, and finally the Otis-Lennon School Ability Test. As the years went by, the term "mental ability" was changed to "school ability" in order to reflect the purpose for which the test is most suitable - that is, to assess examinees' ability to cope with school learning tasks, to suggest their possible placement for school learning functions, and to evaluate their achievement in relation to the talents they bring to school learning.

The latest version of the Otis Lennon School Ability Test® is the Eighth Edition (OLSAT® 8), which is administered in education programs throughout the country in states such as New York, Connecticut, California, Texas, and Virginia.

Content of Fourth and Fifth Grade Test (Level E)

In order to succeed on the OLSAT®, students must perceive accurately and recall what has been perceived, understand patterns and relationships, reason abstract items, and apply generalizations to contexts both new and different. These capabilities are measured through performance on: antonyms, sentence completion, sentence arrangement, arithmetic reasoning, logical selection, word/letter matrix, verbal analogies, verbal classification, inference, figural analogies, pattern matrix, figure series, number series, numeric inference, and number matrix.

Verbal Subtests

The verbal subtests are divided into two groups: verbal comprehension and verbal reasoning. The **verbal comprehension** subtests are designed to measure the student's ability to extrapolate and manipulate information from language. There is an emphasis here on the relational aspects of words and sentences and the nuances of meaning.

There are three type of questions used to test verbal comprehension skills:

1. **Antonyms:** These questions engage the child in searching for the opposite meanings of words. At the foundation of this section are a child's vocabulary skills, however, antonym questions require a high level of comprehension because children will have to understand a concept well enough to reverse it.

2. **Sentence completion:** These questions assess a child's ability to make the logical connections necessary for sentence composition, as they will have to "fill in the blank(s)" with the missing words necessary to create complete and meaningful sentences.

3. **Sentence Arrangement:** Taking the form of a sentence jumble, children must look at a list of words and determine the best possible order they could go in to make a meaningful sentence. These measure the ability of a child to comprehend the structure of language by taking parts and constructing a whole.

The **verbal reasoning** subtests are designed to measure the student's ability to identify and understand patterns and relationships in writing, as well as extrapolate "clues" to aid him/her in solving a problem. There is an emphasis here on skills such as: necessary versus sufficient, similar versus different, and making and applying inferences.

1. **Arithmetic Reasoning:** Arithmetic reasoning incorporates mathematical reasoning into the solving of verbal problems. This section tests basic mathematical reasoning concepts such as counting, quantity, estimation, and inequalities as well as more complex reasoning skills, such as: making inferences and requiring children to solve basic word problems involving addition, subtraction, and simple fractions.

2. **Logical Selection:** These questions ask a student to apply logic in order to find the necessary answer, or the answer that is true in every possible instance, to complete a short statement. This requires a level of focused reasoning as the child considers which answers *could be* correct versus which answer is *always* correct.

3. **Word/Letter Matrix:** In these matrices, the children must be able to identify a relationship between present words or letters in order to supply the missing word or letter. These questions require students to make appropriate inferences and then practically apply them.

4. **Verbal Analogies:** Students will have to find the relationship between a pair of words and then create a second pair using the same relationship rule. Being able to infer relationships is key to success in this section.

5. **Verbal Classifications:** Here students will be looking for the overarching principle that links a set of concepts and then identify the one that does not belong. The key skill in answering these questions is finding the relational quality and evaluating each concept against it.

6. **Inference:** Children will be given an argument and must infer an appropriate conclusion from the premises given. This relies heavily on a student's ability to evaluate the premises and differentiate between necessary and sufficient clauses.

Nonverbal Subtests

The nonverbal subtests are divided into two groups: figural and quantitative reasoning. The **figural reasoning** subtests are designed to measure a student's ability to reason through a visual, or non-language based, medium. There is an emphasis here on inferring relationships, identifying sequences and determining next steps, and making generalizations.

1. **Figural Classifications:** Students will need to identify the overarching principle linking a group of figures and then determine which of the answer choices shares this common attribute. Students will have to carefully evaluate the answer choices and make inferences.

2. **Figural Analogy:** Students will have to find the relationship between a pair of figures and then complete a second pair using the same relationship rule. Being able to infer relationships is key to success in this section.

3. **Pattern Matrix:** Pattern Matrices evaluate the ability of students to find the next step in a geometric series, based on a set of rules. Children need to understand the rule and predict what shape would come next by applying the same rule.

4. **Figural Series:** Figural Series assess the ability to evaluate a sequential series of geometric shapes and to then predict the next occurrence, or simply "what comes next."

The **quantitative reasoning** subtests measure a child's ability to infer patterns and relationships and to solve problems through utilizing numbers, rather than language. In order to be successful, a child will have to be able to predict and establish outcomes based on mathematical processes.

5. **Number Series:** In the same vein as the figural series, children will have to extrapolate a pattern from a sequence of numbers and then apply that pattern to predict what will come next.

6. **Numeric Inference:** Students will have to reason out, using computations skills and rules, why a pair or trio of numbers are related. Once the relationship is established, the student must apply it in order to create another trio or pair.

7. **Number Matrix:** Children must find an overarching principle that links numbers in a matrix and then apply that principle in order to figure out what number is missing.

OLSAT® Practice Test for Fourth and Fifth Grade

OLSAT® Test Structure

The OLSAT® is a multiple choice test. Reading skills are an important component of the fourth and fifth grade exam since the test is entirely self-administered. It is taken in a group where children are required to mark or bubble their answers. The fourth and fifth grade test is utilized for entry or placement into fifth and sixth grade programs.

The OLSAT® content and structure varies for each entry level. The fourth/fifth grade test is 72 questions. These children must answer all 72 questions on the Level E test in a group setting. They have 40 minutes to complete the test.

TABLE 1: Distribution of Types of Questions[1]

SUBTEST	Number of Questions
VERBAL	
Verbal Comprehension	
Antonyms	4
Sentence Completion	4
Sentence Arrangement	4
Verbal Reasoning	
Arithmetic Reasoning	4
Logical Selection	4
Word/ Letter Matrix	4
Verbal Analogies	4
Verbal Classification	4
Inference	4
NONVERBAL	
Figural Reasoning	
Figural Analogies	6
Pattern Matrix	6
Figural Series	6
Quantitative Reasoning	
Number Series	6
Numeric Inference	6
Number Matrix	6

[1] This may or may not represent the question mix of the actual OLSAT® test, as the mix between verbal and nonverbal questions and among different types of questions may change from year to year.

OLSAT® Practice Test for Fourth and Fifth Grade Bright Kids NYC Inc. ©

Scoring Guidelines

The OLSAT® tests comprise a wealth of useful information for test users. Derived scores based on age comparisons and derived scores based on grade comparisons can be provided for Total, Verbal, and Nonverbal raw scores. A raw score, which is defined as the number of questions answered correctly, does not provide enough information about the quality of student performance. The scaled score system connects all test levels and yields a continuous scale that can be used to compare the performance of students taking different levels of the same content cluster. Scaled scores are especially useful for comparing results from the same content cluster across levels, for evaluating changes in performance over time, and for out-of-level testing. Scaled scores can also be translated into percentile ranks.

For example, some New York City Gifted and Talented Programs only provide percentile ranks for the overall combined score, while other districts in the country provide more detailed information. Since the test changes from year to year, the number of questions a child can answer correctly to obtain a specific scaled score will vary based on that particular test's curve and distribution.

The Bright Kids NYC OLSAT® Practice Test can be scored only based on the total number of correct answers, or the overall raw score. Because this practice test has not been standardized with the OLSAT®, scaled scores or percentile ranks cannot be obtained from the raw score. Please realize that a child can miss many questions on the test and still obtain a high score. Thus, it is important that this practice test be utilized as a learning tool to help evaluate a child's strengths and weaknesses rather than to estimate a scaled score or a percentile rank.

General Administration Guidelines

Approximately one hour is required in order to administer the fourth and fifth grade OLSAT® exam. Students need to take around 10 minutes to fill out their personal/identification information on the answer document and test booklet. Then the proctor will review five sample questions in order to familiarize students with the question types. This also takes around 10 minutes. Children will then have 40 minutes to complete 72 questions. The breakdown looks like this:

Identification Information   Approximately 8-10 minutes

Examples   Approximately 8-10 minutes

Test Administration   40 minutes

OLSAT® Practice Test for Fourth and Fifth Grade   Bright Kids NYC Inc. ©

Getting Ready

Materials

1. Children's test booklet removed from this book.

2. Several No. 2 soft lead pencils, erasers, and pencil sharpeners.

3. Ideally, a "Do Not Disturb" sign for the room where you will be administering the test.

4. Clock or a stopwatch.

Prior to Testing

1. Familiarize yourself with the test and the instructions.

2. Provide satisfactory physical conditions in the room where the child will be taking the test. Make sure that there is ample lighting and ventilation. Make sure that the table is clutter free and that the child can sit comfortably.

3. To prevent interruptions, give the child the test when there are no other distractions in the house. If the house is not suitable, try to find a local library or a school.

During Testing

1. Help the child to make sure that they know how to accurately mark the answers by utilizing the sample questions.

2. Adhere to the timing guidelines. Give your child *exactly* 40 minutes to complete the test.

3. Do not give the child any feedback during testing. Discuss the answers only after the testing is complete.

OLSAT® Practice Test for Fourth and Fifth Grade

Instructions

Put the booklet in front of the child and instruct him or her to keep the booklet closed until you are both ready to start. Make sure there are at least two sharpened pencils and an eraser ready. Also, prepare to begin timing the student once he or she begins working on the test.

Sample Question Administration

SAMPLE A

SAY: **Open your booklet to the sample problems on the first page. In Sample A, the first two figures go together in a certain way. Which figure goes with the third figure in the same way?**

Pause while the child looks for the correct figure.

SAY: **Did you choose answer D? In this sample, the innermost shape moves to its opposite from the first shape to the second shape. So, since the small circle is on the left side in the third shape, the correct answer is D, where the small circle is on the right side. Do you understand?**

SAMPLE B

SAY: **Now look at Sample B. Read the question silently and mark down your answer on your answer document.**

Pause while the child looks for the answer.

SAY: **The correct answer is C. The pattern here is to add 4 then subtract 1, progressing from left to right. So, the missing number is 26.**

SAMPLE C

SAY: **Now look at Sample C. Read the question silently and mark down your answer on your answer document.**

Pause while the child looks for the answer.

SAY: **The correct answer is B. Just as foot is to sneaker, hand is to glove. Do you have any questions at this point?**

SAMPLE D

SAY: **Now look at Sample D. Read the question silently and mark down your answer on your answer document.**

Pause while the child looks for the answer.

Sample Question Administration (Continued)

SAY: **The correct answer is A. The figure is rotating 90 degrees clockwise with each figure and the circle is changing from light to dark as the series progresses. Do you understand?**

SAMPLE E

SAY: **Now look at Sample E. Read the question silently and mark down your answer on your answer document.**

Pause while the child looks for the answer.

SAY: **The correct answer is E. Just as tow became stow by adding one letter to it, bit will become bite. Are you comfortable with why bite is the correct answer?**

When all questions have been sufficiently answered,

SAY: **You are to complete the rest of the problems in this book in the same way we have done the sample questions. Read each question carefully and make sure to choose the best answer. Make sure to mark all of your answers on the correct line of your answer sheet. You will have forty minutes to complete the test. You are not expected to answer every question, but try to get through as many as you can. If you are having trouble with a problem, skip it and go on to the next one. When you come to the end of the page, continue on until the end of the test booklet. If you finish before time is up, go back and work on any questions that you skipped or check the ones that you've already completed. Do you have any questions?**

When all questions have been sufficiently answered,

SAY: **Now, you may begin working.**

Make sure that you begin timing as the child commences the test and watch it carefully. At the end of 40 minutes,

SAY: **Stop working now. Put down your pencils and close your booklet.**

OLSAT® Practice Test for Fourth and Fifth Grade

Bright Kids NYC Inc. ©

Bright Kids NYC
OLSAT® Practice Test

Children's Booklet

Fourth and Fifth Grade

Level E

OLSAT® Practice Test for Fourth and Fifth Grade

SAMPLE QUESTIONS

A.

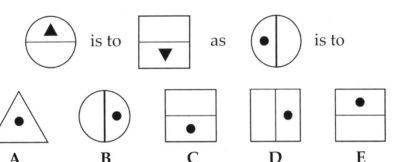

| A | B | C | D | E |

B.

What number is missing in this series?

16 20 19 23 22 **?** 25 29 28

A. 23   **B.** 21   **C.** 26   **D.** 22   **E.** 27

C.

Foot is to **sneaker,** as **hand** is to:

a. scarf   **b.** glove   **c.** sweater   **d.** pants   **e.** earring

D.

The drawings below form a series. Which drawing continues that series and goes where you see the question mark?

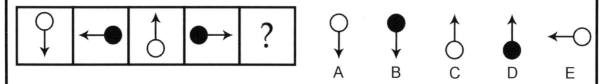

E.

The words in the box go together in a certain way. Which word goes where you see the question mark?

or	for	fore
it	bit	?

A. bitten　**B.** bate　**C.** blink　**D.** bitter　**E.** bite

1.

The opposite of **begin** is:

A. start   B. end   C. move   D. final   E. stop

2.

The drawings in the box go together in a certain way. Which drawing goes where you see the question mark?

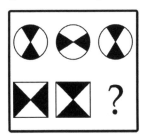

A   B   C   D   E

3.

The numbers in the box go together in a certain way. Which number goes where you see the question mark?

24	16	8
20	12	?

A. 7   B. 5   C. 4   D. 10   E. 9

4.

Which word does **not** go with the others?

A. motorcycle   B. bicycle   C. truck   D. car   E. train

5.

The drawings below form a series. Which drawing continues that series and goes where you see the question mark?

  A   B   C   D   E

6.

Choose the words that **best** complete this sentence.
Don't forget to _____ the present you _____.

A. buy – found
B. wash – sold
C. wrap – bought
D. open – gave
E. throw – got

7.

What number is four less than five times six?

    A. 30   **B.** 20   **C.** 34   **D.** 26   **E.** 28

8.

Dog is to **husky**, as **bird** is to:

    a. hawk   **b.** chirp   **c.** nest   **d.** tree   **e.** mouse

9.

If the words were arranged to make the **best** sentence, with which letter would the **last** word of the sentence begin?

mine	put	to	your	next	book

A. M **B.** P **C.** T **D.** Y **E.** B

10.

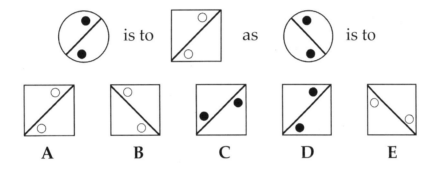

| A | B | C | D | E |

11.

Every classroom has:

A. chalk **B.** blackboard **C.** students **D.** books **E.** pencils

12.

What number is missing in this series?

24 30 25 30 **?** 30 27 30

A. 23 **B.** 30 **C.** 27 **D.** 22 **E.** 26

13.

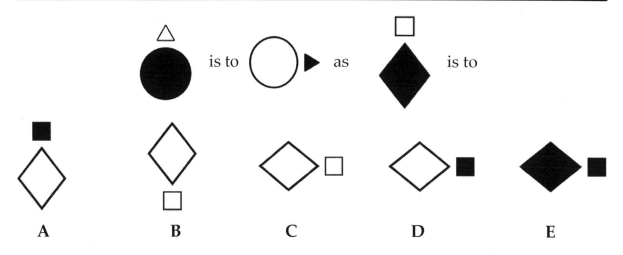

| A | B | C | D | E |

14.

Which word does **not** belong with the others?

A. toaster   **B.** oven   **C.** microwave   **D.** rice cooker   **E.** refrigerator

15.

The opposite of **leave** is:

A. arrive   **B.** stand   **C.** come   **D.** go   **E.** move

16.

The drawings in the box go together in a certain way. Which drawing goes where you see the question mark?

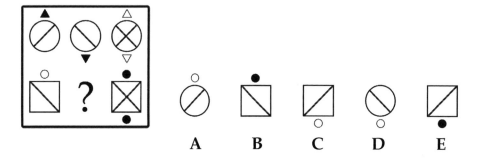

17.

The numbers in the box go together in a certain way. Which number goes where you see the question mark?

2	8	32
3	12	?
4	16	64

A. 42   **B.** 48   **C.** 34   **D.** 60   **E.** 36

18.

The words in the box go together in a certain way. Which word goes where you see the question mark?

| panic | painter | pancake |
| blurry | ? | blatant |

A. buzzing   **B.** berry   **C.** blizzard   **D.** porter   **E.** pale

19.

The numbers in each box go together following the **same** rule. Figure out that rule and then apply it to the third box. What number goes where you see the question mark?

| 6, 3 | | 8, 4 | | 10, ? |

A. 9   **B.** 8   **C.** 5   **D.** 20   **E.** 12

20.

Mary has fewer dolls than Cassie or Olivia, but more dolls than Ann. If Mary has ten dolls, we know for certain that:

A. Ann is trying to give away dolls
B. Cassie and Olivia each have at least twelve dolls
C. Cassie and Olivia have a different number of dolls
D. All of the girls like to play with their dolls
E. Ann has less than ten dolls

21.

The drawings below form a series. Which drawing continues that series and goes where you see the question mark?

22.

Colony is to **ants** as:

A. Wolf is to pack
B. Cub is to lion
C. Hive is to bee
D. Swan is to lake
E. Apple is to pear

23.

Katrina has twelve different books in a box. Some are fiction books and others are non-fiction books. If Katrina has twice as many fiction books as non-fiction books, how many non-fiction books does she have?

A. 10   B. 6   C. 8   D. 4   E. 2

24.

Choose the words that **best** complete the sentence.

The _____ was crowded, so the seats were _____.

A. theater – clean
B. plane – empty
C. train – taken
D. stadium – wet
E. airport – soft

25.

If the words were arranged to make the **best** sentence, with which letter would the **last** word of the sentence begin?

| lock | remember | door | to | front | your |

A. T   B. Y   C. R   D. D   E. L

26.

A student cannot study without:

A. A teacher
B. Books
C. Reading
D. Going to school
E. Trying

27.

What comes next in the series?

2 1 A 1 3 Z 4 1 C 1 5 **?**

A. A   B. 1   C. 6   D. Y   E. X

28.

The drawings below form a series. Which drawing continues that series and goes where you see the question mark?

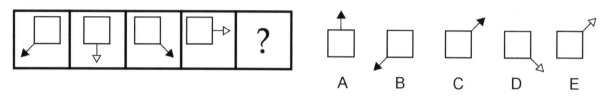

29.

The numbers in the box go together. Which number goes where you see the question mark?

2	6	18
3	9	27
4	12	?

A. 16   **B.** 48   **C.** 36   **D.** 24   **E.** 30

30.

The drawings in the box go together. Which drawing goes where you see the question mark?

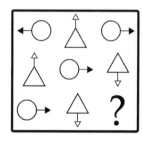

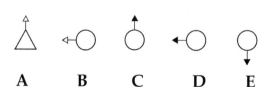

31.

The numbers in the box go together. Which numbers go where you see the question mark?

1,4	3,2	1,3,4,2
6,9	?	6,8,9,7

A. 9,7   **B.** 8,9   **C.** 8,7   **D.** 6,7   **E.** 7,8

32.

The opposite of **translucent** is:

A. clear   **B.** opaque   **C.** transparent   **D.** solid   **E.** light

33.

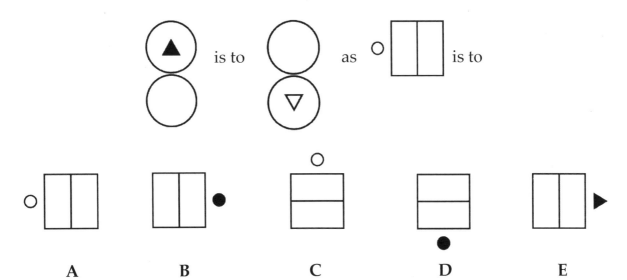

34.

Mark bought more marbles than Joshua or Andrew, but fewer than Michael. If Mark bought six blue marbles and two red marbles, then we know:

A. Mark likes red marbles the least
B. Andrew has the largest marble collection
C. Michael bought at least nine marbles
D. Andrew and Michael bought the same number of marbles
E. Joshua spent the most money on marbles

35.

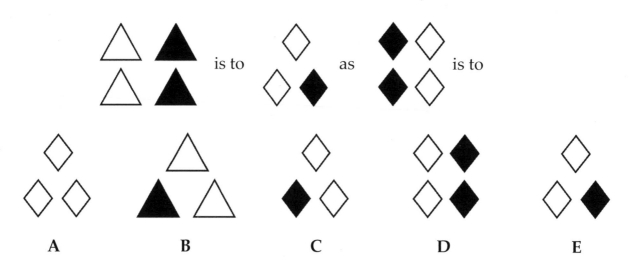

36.

The numbers in each box go together following the **same** rule. Figure out that rule and then apply it to the third box. What number goes where you see the question mark?

| 3, 18 | 5, 30 | 7, ? |

A. 42   **B.** 40   **C.** 49   **D.** 36   **E.** 38

37.

Which word does **not** go with the others?

A. crop   **B.** crisp   **C.** crack   **D.** crew   **E.** cork

38.

The numbers in each box go together following the **same** rule. Figure out that rule and then apply it to the third box. What number goes where you see the question mark?

$$\boxed{3, 2, 8} \qquad \boxed{4, 3, 12} \qquad \boxed{5, 4, ?}$$

A. 13   **B.** 16   **C.** 18   **D.** 15   **E.** 20

39.

The drawings in the box go together in a certain way. Which drawing goes where you see the question mark?

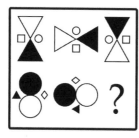

    A   B   C   D   E

40.

The numbers in the box go together in a certain way. Which number goes where you see the question mark?

14	21	28
18	25	?

A. 32   **B.** 35   **C.** 21   **D.** 31   **E.** 33

41.

The drawings below form a series. Which drawing continues that series and goes where you see the question mark?

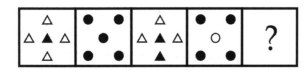

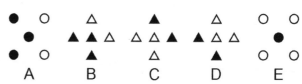

42.

What number is four more than nine times four?

A. 36   **B.** 42   **C.** 40   **D.** 32   **E.** 44

43.

People who are in a building will always be:

A. working   **B.** eating   **C.** walking   **D.** inside   **E.** looking outside

44.

Carl is taller than George, who is taller than John, but shorter than Mark. We know for certain that:

A. Carl is taller than Mark
B. John and Mark are the same height
C. John is the shortest child
D. Mark is the oldest child
E. Carl and John are almost the same height

45.

What comes next in the series?

22 L 24 O 26 R 28 **?**

A. V   **B.** U   **C.** S   **D.** 30   **E.** 32

46.

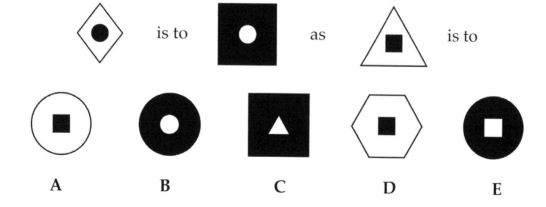

A   B   C   D   E

47.

If the words were arranged to make the **best** sentence, with which letter would the **second** word of the sentence begin?

| boxed | to | forget | do | pack | your | not | lunch |

A. N   **B.** D   **C.** P   **D.** Y   **E.** B

48.

The numbers in each box go together following the **same** rule. Figure out that rule and then apply it to the third box. What number goes where you see the question mark?

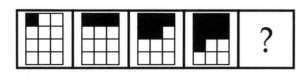

A. 4   **B.** 8   **C.** 5   **D.** 7   **E.** 9

49.

The drawings below form a series. Which drawing continues that series and goes where you see the question mark?

A   B   C   D   E

50.

Choose the word that **best** completes the sentence.

On her first day of work, the mayor talked about the _____ mayor's contributions.

    A. previous
    B. new
    C. wise
    D. young
    E. generous

51.

The drawings in the box go together in a certain way. Which drawing goes where you see the question mark?

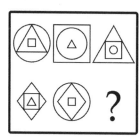

    A   **B**   **C**   **D**   **E**

52.

The numbers in the box go together in a certain way. Which number goes where you see the question mark?

6	12	18
12	18	24
18	24	?

A. 36   **B.** 28   **C.** 30   **D.** 18   **E.** 24

53.

What comes next in the series?

H 30 I 32 J 28 K 30 L **?**

A. 32   **B.** 26   **C.** 34   **D.** 29   **E.** 28

54.

The words in the box go together in a certain way. Which word goes where you see the question mark?

at	bat	bate
on	con	**?**

A. cant   **B.** scone   **C.** cone   **D.** icon   **E.** knot

55.

The numbers in each box go together following the same rule. Figure out that rule and then apply it to the third box. What number goes where you see the question mark?

10, 5, 2   14, 7, 4   18, ?, 6

A. 5   **B.** 9   **C.** 11   **D.** 7   **E.** 3

56.

Kitten is to **cat** as **fowl** is to:

A. sheep   B. lamb   C. horse   D. cow   E. pig

57.

Choose the word that **best** completes the sentence.

The directions to the airport were _____, therefore we missed our flight home.

    A. right
    B. confusing
    C. clear
    D. convenient
    E. correct

58.

Catherine has 16 ribbons. Some of her ribbons are solid colored ribbons, others are striped ribbons. If she has three times as many striped ribbons as solid colored ones, how many solid colored ribbons does she have?

    A. 7   **B.** 4   **C.** 12   **D.** 8   **E.** 2

59.

Last week, Penny went to the store more often than Sam, but not as often as Cynthia. If Cynthia went to the store on Monday, Wednesday, and Sunday, then we know for certain that:

    A. Cynthia didn't go anywhere on Tuesday and Thursday
    B. Penny went to the store one or two days
    C. Sam's mom usually goes to the store without him
    D. Sam only went to the store one day
    E. Penny went to the store on Thursday and Saturday

60.

The opposite of **pompous** is:

    A. timid   **B.** popular   **C.** modest   **D.** foolish   **E.** demanding

61.

Which word does **not** go with the others?

A. watch   **B.** look   **C.** stare   **D.** dose   **E.** gaze

62.

The drawings in the box go together in a certain way. Which drawing goes where you see the question mark?

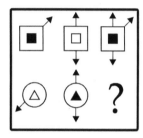 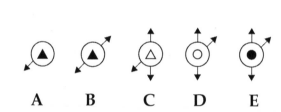

            A   B   C   D   E

63.

63.   If the words were arranged to make the **best** sentence, with which letter would the **first** word of the sentence begin?

notebook   the   cooking   in   directions   my   read

A. T   **B.** R   **C.** D   **D.** C   **E.** N

64.

The numbers in the box go together in a certain way. Which number goes where you see the question mark?

4	13	22
8	17	?

A. 27   **B.** 26   **C.** 31   **D.** 29   **E.** 31

65.

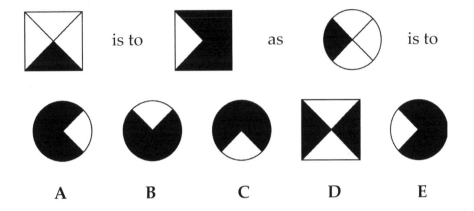

A   B   C   D   E

66.

An orchestra cannot play music without:

A. Lyrics
B. Conductor
C. Instruments
D. Trumpets
E. Pianos

67.

The words in the box go together in a certain way. Which word goes where you see the question mark?

are	care	scare
ore	tore	?

A. score   **B.** store   **C.** tire   **D.** scone   **E.** satire

68.

The numbers in each box go together following the **same** rule. Figure out that rule and then apply it to the third box. What number goes where you see the question mark?

| 2, 1 | | 4, 2 | | 6, ? | **A.** 2   **B.** 3   **C.** 4   **D.** 12   **E.** 8

69.

The drawings below form a series. Which drawing continues that series and goes where you see the question mark?

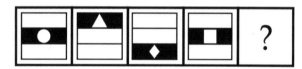 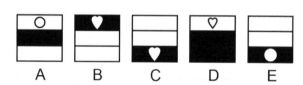

70.

Remember is to **forget** as:

A. close is to near
B. build is to built
C. start is to stopping
D. give is to take
E. bought is to buyer

71.

What number comes next in the series?

3 9 6 12 9 15 ?

A. 6   B. 10   C. 12   D. 18   E. 8

72.

What number comes next in the series?

2 6 3 9 4 12 5 **?**

A. 20　　**B.** 15　　**C.** 25　　**D.** 30　　**E.** 6

OLSAT® Practice Test for Fourth and Fifth Grade   Bright Kids NYC Inc. ©

Answer Key

NUMBER	CORRECT ANSWER	CHILD'S ANSWER	TYPE OF QUESTION
1.	B		Antonym
2.	A		Pattern Matrix
3.	C		Number Matrix
4.	E		Verbal Classification
5.	E		Figural Series
6.	C		Sentence Completion
7.	D		Arithmetic Reasoning
8.	A		Verbal Analogy
9.	A		Sentence Arrangement
10.	B		Figural Analogy
11.	C		Logical Selection
12.	E		Number Series
13.	D		Figural Analogy
14.	E		Verbal Classification
15.	A		Antonym
16.	C		Pattern Matrix
17.	B		Number Matrix
18.	C		Word Matrix
19.	C		Number Series
20.	E		Inference
21.	B		Figural Series
22.	C		Verbal Analogy
23.	D		Arithmetic Reasoning
24.	C		Sentence Completion
25.	D		Sentence Arrangement
26.	E		Logical Selection
27.	E		Number Series
28.	C		Figural Series
29.	C		Number Matrix
30.	D		Pattern Matrix

Answer Key (Continued)

NUMBER	CORRECT ANSWER	CHILD'S ANSWER	TYPE OF QUESTION
31.	C		Number Series
32.	B		Antonym
33.	B		Figural Analogy
34.	C		Inference
35.	B		Picture Analogy
36.	A		Number Series
37.	E		Verbal Classification
38.	B		Number Series
39.	D		Pattern Matrix
40.	A		Number Matrix
41.	B		Pattern Series
42.	C		Arithmetic Reasoning
43.	D		Logical Selection
44.	C		Inference
45.	B		Number Series
46.	E		Figural Analogy
47.	A		Sentence Arrangement
48.	C		Number Series
49.	C		Figural Series
50.	A		Sentence Completion
51.	E		Pattern Matrix
52.	C		Number Matrix
53.	B		Number Series
54.	C		Word Matrix
55.	B		Number Series
56.	C		Verbal Analogy
57.	B		Sentence Completion
58.	B		Arithmetic Reasoning
59.	B		Inference
60.	C		Antonym

Answer Key (Continued)

NUMBER	CORRECT ANSWER	CHILD'S ANSWER	TYPE OF QUESTION
61.	D		Verbal Classification
62.	C		Pattern Matrix
63.	B		Sentence Arrangement
64.	B		Number Matrix
65.	B		Figural Analogy
66.	C		Logical Selection
67.	B		Word Matrix
68.	B		Number Series
69.	B		Figural Series
70.	D		Verbal Analogy
71.	C		Number Series
72.	B		Number Series

Answers Explained

1. Correct Answer: B

Here we are looking for the *best* answer. Immediately <u>start</u> and <u>move</u> should be eliminated as answers. <u>Start</u> is the same as begin and <u>move</u> is neither the same nor different. <u>Final</u> is incorrect because of the part of speech; it is an adjective, or a descriptive word, while <u>begin</u> is a verb, or an action word. This leaves <u>stop</u> and <u>end</u>. Both are good choices, but <u>end</u> is the *best* answer because of opposite pairings. The opposite of stop is start, not begin.

2. Correct Answer: A

The pattern in the top row shows the shaded portions of the circle rotating ninety degrees as we progress from left to right. That same pattern must be applied to the second row in order to find the best answer. Immediately, we can eliminate answers <u>C</u> and <u>D</u> because they are circles and the figures in the second row are squares. <u>A</u> is the correct answer because the highlighted portions are opposite one another and have rotated one space from where they were in the prior square.

3. Correct Answer: C

The pattern in the box shows that we are subtracting eight as we move from left to right in each row. For example, in the first row, the numbers are 24, 16, and 8. (**24**-8=**16**-8=**8**). Therefore, the answer is 4, because 12-8=4.

4. Correct Answer: E

Here we are looking for the word that does *not* belong with the others. All of our choices are modes of transportation, which can be confusing. However, a <u>train</u> is the only choice available that is not a personal mode of transportation. Families can own a <u>car</u>, <u>truck</u>, <u>bicycle</u> or <u>motorcycle</u>, but not a <u>train</u>.

5. Correct Answer: E

In this series, the key is to pay attention to the highlighted portions of the figures. The pattern is as follows: shaded innermost shape, shaded middle shape, shaded outermost shape, repeat. Once the pattern is identified, answer choices <u>A</u>, <u>C</u>, and <u>D</u> can be eliminated. Now, one must look at the shapes. The pattern of the shapes is circle, square, diamond. Therefore, the answer is <u>E</u>.

6. Correct Answer: C

When answering this question, it is very important to place the words into the corresponding blank spaces and then read the complete sentence. Does it make sense? The one that makes the most sense will be the *best* sentence and the right answer. You wouldn't <u>open the present you gave</u>, nor would you be reminded to <u>throw the present you got</u> or <u>wash the present you sold</u>. So, eliminate answer choices <u>B</u>, <u>D</u> and <u>E</u>. If you <u>found</u> a present, you wouldn't need to <u>buy</u> it. So, that leaves answer choice <u>C</u>.

7. Correct Answer: D

"Four less than five times six" is asking the student to multiply five and six (thirty) and then subtract four from the total. Written as a traditional math equation, it would look like this: $(5 \times 6) - 4 = 26$.

8. Correct Answer: A

The sample analogy is comparing a dog to a husky. It is taking an animal and comparing it to a specific breed or type of that same animal. The student must apply this logic utilizing a bird instead of a dog. Which answer is a type of bird? Answer choice <u>A</u>, the hawk.

9. Correct Answer: A

In this word jumble, the first step is for the student to make the *best* possible sentence out of the words in the box. That sentence should be: "Put your book next to mine." Once the sentence is established, the student must pick out the last word, "mine." Mine starts with an "M," so the answer is <u>A</u>.

10. Correct Answer: B

In this figural analogy, the student must establish the relationship of the first pair and apply it to the second pair. In this case, the diagonals in the square and circle are pointing in the same direction (i.e. from the lower left corner to the upper right corner) and the small circles are in the same position. So, you can eliminate any answer choice where the diagonal is pointing in the direction opposite to that of the third circle; answers <u>A</u>, <u>C</u>, and <u>D</u>. The correct answer is <u>B</u> because the position of the small circles is the same as the circle in that pairing.

11. Correct Answer: C

It's an important strategy for a student to notice the strength of words in the questions. "Every," "always," and "for certain," are examples of definite words. If a student

encounters one of these words in a question, it means that in any possible scenario this answer will be true. There can never be a scenario when the answer is false. With that in mind, the student can eliminate answer choices. There are many classrooms that no longer use blackboards or chalk, so answer choices A and B can be crossed out. Similarly, there *could* be a class where all the students wrote with pens or typed their notes and no one had any pencils. There *could* be a class in which there were no books. So, answer choices E and D can be eliminated. Answer C is the correct answer because no space would be a classroom unless there were students to learn in it.

12. **Correct Answer: E**

In any series question, the first step is for the student to understand the pattern. In this series, the pattern is as follows: x, 30, y (x+1), 30, z (y+1) 30. The 30's are a distraction. The real pattern is that every other number increase by one. Therefore, the answer is E.

13. **Correct Answer: D**

In this figural analogy, the key observations are the highlighting and the positioning of the shapes. The highlighting alternates from the first to the second shape and the position of the triangle switches from the top to the right side. These are traits that the student will need to apply to the second pair. So, all the answers that do not have the small square on the right side of the diamond can be eliminated (A and B). Now, we need to apply the highlighting rule. The correct answer is D because the highlighting is the opposite of the other figure in the pair.

14. **Correct Answer: E**

All of our answer choices are kitchen appliances, yet four of them heat up food. Therefore, refrigerator, does not belong because it is the only choice that cools food.

15. **Correct Answer: A**

The first step to answering a "choose the opposite" question is to eliminate words that are synonyms, or the same, and words that are irrelevant, neither the same nor different. Under that rule, the student can immediately cross out go, stand, and move. Now the student must consider the *best* possible opposite pairings. The best opposite of come is go. So, that leaves the best possible answer, which is arrive.

16. **Correct Answer: C**

In the top row the diagonals change direction from the first to the second shape. In the first shape, it goes from right to left, with the small triangle on top, and in the second circle it goes from left to right, with the small triangle on the bottom. The third shape

is a mixture of the two, with both diagonals and triangles (not shaded) on the top and bottom. When you apply this pattern to the bottom row, the missing shape should have a diagonal that goes from right to left and a non-shaded circle on bottom. Therefore, the answer is C.

17. Correct Answer: B

The pattern displayed in each row is that the numbers are multiplied by four as we move from left to right. For example, in the first row, the numbers are 2, 8, and 32. **2** x 4 = **8** x 4 =**32**. So, the missing number is going to be the sum of 12 times four, which is 48.

18. Correct Answer: C

Panic, painter, and pancake have something in common. The first two letters of each of the words are "p" and "a." The student must take this relationship and apply it to the second row. The correct answer should start with "bl," the same as blurry and blatant. Therefore, the answer is blizzard.

19. Correct Answer: C

The rule in the first two boxes is that the first number is double the second number. So, when we apply that to the third box, the missing number is 5.

20. Correct Answer: E

Here, it is extremely important for a student to notice the strength of the words "we know for certain." First, a student should eliminate any assumptions, or answers that include anything that we aren't explicitly told by *the question*. For instance, answer choices A, C, and D can be eliminated under that rule. They are assumptions, while the other answer choices are inferences. Next, a student must eliminate the incorrect inferences. If Mary has ten dolls, then Cassie or Olivia could each have eleven dolls. They do not need to have at least twelve. So, answer choice B is a bad inference and incorrect. Answer E is correct because we are told that Ann has less dolls than Mary and that Mary has 10 dolls.

21. Correct Answer: B

It is important to break down each figure in this pattern sequence in order to infer what will come next. The pattern in this series is that the innermost shape becomes the next outermost shape and the arrow moves ninety degrees clockwise from left to right. Since the hexagon is the innermost shape of the fourth figure, we know that the outermost shape of the correct answer must be a hexagon, which eliminates choices A, D, and E. The correct answer is B because the arrow in that figure is pointing downwards, which is the next clockwise progression.

22. Correct Answer: C

In this analogy, the student must find the relationship between "colony" and "ants" and then apply it to the answer choices to see which makes the most sense. A colony is a home to the ants. So, the answer is C because a hive is also a home for bees. The tricky answer here is D, but it is incorrect because a swan is not home to a lake, even though a lake is home to a swan. The order in analogies is incredibly important, so students must learn to pay attention to that.

23. Correct Answer: D

In this math problem, some students will check all of the answers to see which will add up to 12. That will work, but it is time consuming. The ideal response would be to work through the word problem and figure out that the answer will be 12 divided by 3, which is four, answer D.

24. Correct Answer: C

In this sentence completion question, the best answer is the one that makes the most sense. In this case, the answer is C because when the train is crowded the seats are usually taken. Answer choices A and B can be eliminated quickly because if the theater is crowded, it is probably not very clean and if the plane is crowded then the seats would be full, not empty. If the airport is crowded, it does not necessarily follow that the seats will be soft, nor does it follow that if the stadium is crowded the seats will be wet. Those sentences could be true, but they are not the most logical answer.

25. Correct Answer: D

When the sentence jumble is solved, the student should get "Remember to lock your front door." The last word of the sentence is "door." So the answer is D.

26. Correct Answer: E

In this question, the student must figure out which answer choice is necessary for studying. Answer choices A and D can be eliminated because many students study at home, either by themselves or with a parent. So, it is not necessary that a student have a teacher present or be at school. Nor is it necessary for them to have books or be reading (B and C). A student can never study without trying, though. That is necessary, so that is the correct answer.

27. Correct Answer: E

The key to figure out this series is to pay attention to the letters. It's a tricky one because the letters not only skip A to C, but alternate between the beginning and end of the

alphabet. We skip one letter in the first part of the alphabet, so we must skip one on the backside of the alphabet. So, Y is skipped and the answer is X (answer choice E).

28. **Correct Answer: C**

The pattern in this series is that the arrow rotates counterclockwise around the square while the highlighting of the point alternates. Since the arrow is in the middle of the right side of the square and not highlighted, the answer is C, where the arrow is in the top right corner of the square and highlighted.

29. **Correct Answer: C**

The numbers in the box are multiplied by 3 as we move from left to right. For example, in the first row we have 2, 6, and 18. $2 \times 3 = 6 \times 3 = 18$. Therefore, answer choice C is correct because 12 times 3 equals 36.

30. **Correct Answer: D**

In this box, the pattern shows the shapes and highlighting alternate from left to right as the arrow rotates clockwise. So, our answer must be a circle, with the highlighted arrow pointing left. Therefore, the answer is D.

31. **Correct Answer: C**

In the top row, the first two number groups, when each number is added, equal the same number and in the last number group, when the numbers are added, equal double that number. Here's the pattern written out: $1 + 4 = 5$; $3 + 2 = 5$; $1 + 3 + 4 + 2 = 10$. In the bottom row, we know that the same pattern applies since $6 + 9 = 15$ and $6 + 8 + 9 + 7 = 30$. So, the answer will be a number group that equals 15; answer choice C.

32. **Correct Answer: B**

Translucent is an adjective that means being clear, allowing light to pass through. So, the student can immediately eliminate answer choices A and C because they are synonyms, or the same, as translucent. Since something can be solid and translucent, answer choice D is incorrect and because the word "light" is neither the same nor the opposite of translucent, answer choice E can be crossed out. The word "opaque" means impenetrable to light, so answer choice B is the correct answer.

33. **Correct Answer: B**

The pattern in the first pair shows the small shape switches whether or not it is highlighted and moves to the alternate side of the larger shape. Since this is a figure analogy, we must apply this pattern to the second set. Therefore the answer is B.

34. Correct Answer: C

On this question, it is important to eliminate assumptions. Do not apply outside knowledge to questions like this. Whatever facts the student is given in the question must be the only facts applied to finding the answer. We do not know who has the largest marble collection, who spent the most money on marbles, or Mark's color preference. So, answer choices <u>A</u>, <u>B</u> and <u>E</u> can be immediately eliminated. We know that Andrew and Michael did not have the same amount of marbles, so answer choice <u>D</u> is incorrect. <u>C</u> is the correct answer because we are certain that Michael has more marbles than Mark. So, if Mark has eight marbles, Michael must have at least nine.

35. Correct Answer: B

The pattern in the first pair is that the top highlighted triangle is taken away and the shape changes. So, since this is a figure analogy, the student must apply that pattern to the answer choices. The top highlighted shape must be taken away, this time on the left side, and the shapes should change to triangles. Therefore, answer choice <u>B</u> is correct.

36. Correct Answer: A

The pattern in the boxes is that the first number is multiplied by six to get the second number. For instance, in the first box we have 3 and 18. **3 x 6 = 18**. So, the correct answer will be answer choice <u>A</u> because **7 x 6 = 42**.

37. Correct Answer: E

Here a student must look at all of the answer choices and determine what makes four of them similar and one of them different. In this case, the similarity is in the spelling of the word rather than the meaning. Cork is the only word that does not begin with "cr," therefore, answer choice <u>E</u> is correct.

38. Correct Answer: B

The pattern in the first two boxes is that the first number minus one gives us the second number, and that number times four gives us the third number. In the first box we have 3, 2, and 8. **3 – 1 = 2 x 4 = 8**. When we apply this pattern to the third box, we know that the missing number will be the product of four times four. Therefore, the answer is 16, answer choice <u>B</u>.

39. Correct Answer: D

In the box, the objects are rotating. In the top row, the shapes move clockwise as we progress from left to right and in the bottom row they move counterclockwise. The

figure that represents a counterclockwise rotation of the figure is D.

40. **Correct Answer: A**

The pattern in the box is that we are adding seven to each number as we move from left to right. For example, the numbers in the top row are 14, 21, 28. **14 + 7 = 21 + 7 = 28.** So, if the student applies this pattern to the second row, the answer must be the sum of twenty-five and seven, which is thirty-two (answer choice A).

41. **Correct Answer: B**

Here, the triangle figures are adding a shaded shape as we move from left to right and the circular figures are taking one away. Since the design is alternating triangle and circles, we know that the missing figure must be a triangle one. So, the student can eliminate all the circle figures immediately. The correct answer is B because that follows the pattern of shading in an additional triangle.

42. **Correct Answer: C**

In order to find the correct answer, the student must multiply nine and four and then add four to the product. Written out mathematically is should look like this: (9 x 4) + 4 = 40. It is important to add the four after the multiplication takes place.

43. **Correct Answer: D**

This is an "always" question, which means that we are looking for an answer that could never be false. It is important to notice strong words like "always" and "every" in testing. Answer choices A, B, C, and E could be true, but they are not *always* true. A person could be looking out a window, or eating, or working, or walking, but they are not likely to *always* do that when in a building. On the flipside, when people are in a building, they are *always* inside no matter what else they may be doing.

44. **Correct Answer: C**

On these types of questions it is important to remember that the only facts that can be applied to finding the answer are given to you in the question. Eliminate first any answer choices that are assumptions. Answer choices A, D, and E are good examples of assumptions because they are not supported by facts in the question. We have no way of knowing if Carl is taller than Mark, or if Mark is the oldest, or if Carl and John are almost the same height. We know that answer B is incorrect because we are told that George is taller than John and shorter than Mark, so John and Mark could not be the same height. Answer choice C is correct because we know that Carl and Mark are taller than George and that George is taller than John. Therefore, John is the shortest.

45. Correct Answer: B

The numbers in this series are moving upwards by two as we move from left to right. Similarly, the letters are skipping two in alphabetical order as we move in that same direction. Written out: **L M̶ N̶ O P Q̶ R S̶ T̶ U.** As you can see, the correct answer is U because you are skipping S and T in order to continue the pattern.

46. Correct Answer: E

In the first pair, the larger shape switches and the highlighting alternates from the inner shape to the outer shape, with the inner shape remaining a circle. This is a figural analogy, so we must apply that pattern to the second pair. Therefore, the answer is E because the outer shape changes but the inner shape remains the same, and the highlighting alternates from the inner shape to the outer shape.

47. Correct Answer: A

In this sentence jumble, the student must create the best possible sentence by putting the words in the box in order. The sentence should be "Do not forget to pack your boxed lunch." The second word in the sentence is "not," which begins with an N. Therefore, the answer is A.

48. Correct Answer: C

The pattern in the first two boxes is that the first number minus one equals the second number. That number plus five equals the third number. For example, in the first box, the numbers are 2, 1, 6. **2 − 1 = 1 + 5 = 6.** When the student applies this rule to the third box, the missing number is five.

49. Correct Answer: C

In each of the boxes, the numbers progress from left to right by adding two. There are one, three, five, and seven blocks shaded in each of the squares respectively. The student is looking for the square that has nine blocks shaded and follows the pattern. Both C and D have nine blocks shaded, but C follows the pattern of filling in blocks across the rows, rather than vertically. So, C is the correct answer.

50. Correct Answer: A

The student must pick the answer that makes the *most* sense when inserted into the sentence. It's important to read the whole sentence to put your answer in context. For instance, the most important part of the sentence is "On her first day of work, the mayor…" Here we learn that she has just taken over as mayor, so answer choice B is wrong because

she *is* the new mayor. When choosing, it makes the most sense that she would be talking about the previous mayor. So, answer choice <u>A</u> is correct.

51. **Correct Answer: E**

In the top row, the student should take note of the fact that none of the outermost, innermost, or middle shapes are the same in any of the figures. The student should take this observation and apply it to the second row. The outermost shapes in the second row are a diamond and a circle. Since we know that these will not repeat, we can eliminate answer choices <u>A</u>, <u>B</u>, and <u>C</u>. Answer <u>D</u> is incorrect because the middle shape is a diamond, just like the second figure in that grouping. The shapes should not repeat, therefore it must be eliminated. Answer <u>E</u> is correct because none of the shapes are repeated.

52. **Correct Answer: C**

The pattern in this box is that we are adding six to each number as we move from left to right. For example, the numbers in the top row are 6, 12, 18. **6 + 6 = 12 + 6 = 18**. Applying this pattern to the third row, the missing number is thirty, answer choice <u>C</u>.

53. **Correct Answer: B**

In this series, the letters progress alphabetically. The numbers are a bit trickier. Here is the pattern written out mathematically without the letters:

$$30 \ (+2) \ 32 \ (-4) \ 28 \ (+2) \ 30 \ (-4) \ \textbf{?} = \textbf{26}$$

The correct answer is 26.

54. **Correct Answer: C**

In the top row, as we progress from left to right, one letter is being added to make new words. At gains a "b" and becomes bat, which gains an "e" and becomes bate. To follow this pattern, one letter needs to be added to con to become a new word. Therefore, the answer is "cone," choice <u>C</u>.

55. **Correct Answer: B**

The rule in the boxes is that the first number, divided by two, equals the second number. That number minus three equals the third number. For example, the numbers in the first grouping are 10, 5, and 2. **10 / 2 = 5 -3 = 2**. When we apply that to the third box, the missing number is found to be 9.

56. Correct Answer: C

In this analogy question, the student must find the relationship of the first pairing and apply that relationship to the second pairing. A kitten is a baby cat. So we know that a fowl must be what we call a baby of another animal type. A fowl is a baby horse, so the answer is <u>C</u>.

57. Correct Answer: B

Here, the student is looking for the word that makes the most sense when inserted into the sentence. The most important part of the sentence is the end: "therefore we missed our flight." So, the directions must have been bad if they were the reason that these travelers missed their flight. Immediately the student can eliminate answer choices <u>A</u>, <u>C</u>, <u>D</u>, and <u>E</u>. These would all make the directions stronger. The only negative adjective among the answer choices is <u>confusing</u>, so it is the correct answer.

58. Correct Answer: B

In this math problem, some students will check all of the answers to see which will add up to 16. That will work, but it is time consuming. The ideal response would be to work through the word problem and figure out that the answer will be 16 divided by 4, which is four, answer <u>B</u>.

59. Correct Answer: B

First, notice the strength of the words "for certain" in this question. On these types of questions it is important to remember that the only facts that can be applied to finding the answer are given to you in the question. Eliminate first any answer choices that are assumptions. Answers <u>A</u>, <u>C</u>, and <u>E</u> are good examples of assumptions. We are not told anything about Sam's mom, what days Penny goes to the store, or what Cynthia does or doesn't do on days when she's not at the store. We can cross out answer <u>D</u> because while it could be true, we cannot be certain that it is true. Sam could have gone to the store only once, or he could have not gone at all. We are certain that Penny went to the store once or twice, because she went less than Cynthia, who went three times, and more than Sam (meaning she had to go at least once).

60. Correct Answer: C

Pompous means to be arrogant and to boast about yourself. The opposite of being pompous is to be <u>modest</u>. Though pompous people are rarely timid, they are not necessarily opposite traits.

61. Correct Answer: D

Here a student must look at all of the answer choices and determine what makes four of them similar and one of them different. Watch, look, stare, and gaze are all related because in every case someone is seeing something. However, when someone is dozing, they are closing their eyes and falling asleep. Therefore, "doze" is the one that doesn't belong.

62. Correct Answer: C

In the top row of this box the first two figures combine to form the third one. The arrows are a combination of the first two shapes, with the inner square shaded the same as it is in the first figure. The answer is C because the arrows on that figure are a combination of the first two figures in the bottom row and the inner triangle is not shaded, the same as in the first figure.

63. Correct Answer: B

In this word jumble, the first step is for the student to make the *best* possible sentence out of the words in the box. That sentence should be: "Read the cooking directions in my notebook." The first word in the sentence is "read." Therefore, the letter the question is looking for is R.

64. Correct Answer: B

The pattern in the box is that we are adding nine to each number as we progress from left to right. For example, the numbers in the first row are 4, 13, and 22. $4 + 9 = 13 + 9 = 22$. When we apply this rule to the second line, the missing number is twenty-six.

65. Correct Answer: B

In this figural analogy, the student must take the relationship between the first two shapes and apply it to the second pairing. The first figure has one shaded section and the second figure has that same section shaded, plus two sections to the right (or clockwise). B is the correct answer because the shaded section in the first figure is also shaded, as well as the two sections to its right (or clockwise).

66. Correct Answer: C

The student must look for the person or thing that is necessary to an orchestra for it to play. Most orchestral music is not accompanied by singing, so lyrics (answer choice A) can be eliminated. An orchestra can still play without a trumpet or pianos and even if the conductor isn't present. However, it is necessary for an orchestra to have instruments in order to have something to play.

67. Correct Answer: B

In the first row, as we move from left to right, a single letter is being added to each word to make a new word. Are + C = care + S= scare. The correct answer will add one letter to "tore" and make a new word. Therefore, the correct answer is <u>B</u>: store.

68. Correct Answer: B

The student must find the rule utilized in the first two boxes and apply it to the third box. The rule is that the first number, divided by two equals the second number. When applied to the first number in the third box, we find that the missing number is 3. **6 / 2 = 3**.

69. Correct Answer: B

Here, the shaded area moves from the middle square to the top square to the bottom square to the middle square again. The inner shapes move with the shading, but never repeats. So, the correct answer will have the top square shaded and include an inner shape that has not been presented. Therefore, the answer is <u>B</u>.

70. Correct Answer: D

In this analogy, the student must find the relationship between the first pair of words and identify another pair that has the same relationship. Remember and forget are opposites. So, the correct answer will also be a pair of opposites. Therefore, the answer is <u>D</u>.

71. Correct Answer: C

The pattern here is that we are adding six and subtracting three alternatively as we move from left to right. Written out:

$$3 \ (+6) \ 9 \ (-3) \ 6 \ (+6) \ 12 \ (-3) \ 9 \ (+6) \ 15 \ (-3) \ \textbf{? = 12}$$

Therefore, the answer is <u>12</u>.

72. Correct Answer: B

The pattern here is that we are multiplying every other number by three and then subtracting an odd number, progressively increasing by 2, from the product. Here it is written out:

$$2 \ (x3) \ 6 \ (-3) \ 3 \ (x3) \ 9 \ (-5) \ 4 \ (x3) \ 12 \ (-7) \ 5 \ (x3) \ \textbf{? = 15}$$

Therefore, the answer is <u>15</u>.